GOLF RULES
& ETIQUETTE
SIMPLIFIED

GOLF RULES & ETIQUETTE SIMPLIFIED

REVISED & UPDATED THIRD EDITION

What You Need to Know to Walk the Links Like a Pro

JOHN COMPANIOTTE

FOREWORDS BY RAYMOND FLOYD AND BY LOUISE SUGGS

New York   Chicago   San Francisco   Lisbon   London   Madrid   Mexico City
Milan   New Delhi   San Juan   Seoul   Singapore   Sydney   Toronto

The **McGraw·Hill** Companies

Copyright © 2012 by The McGraw-Hill Companies, Inc. All rights reserved. Printed in the United States of America. Except as permitted under the United States Copyright Act of 1976, no part of this publication may be reproduced or distributed in any form or by any means, or stored in a database or retrieval system, without the prior written permission of the publisher.

1 2 3 4 5 6 7 8 9 10   QFR/QFR   1 9 8 7 6 5 4 3 2

ISBN   978-0-07-179736-8
MHID   0-07-179736-X

e-ISBN 978-0-07-179737-5
e-MHID   0-07-179737-8

Interior photographs by Warren Grant

McGraw-Hill products are available at special quantity discounts to use as premiums and sales promotions or for use in corporate training programs. To contact a representative, please e-mail us at bulksales@mcgraw-hill.com.

Excerpts from *The Rules of Golf* are reprinted from *The Rules of Golf 2012–2015* ©2011 United States Golf Association, with permission. All rights reserved.

The Rules of Golf, which were effective as of January 1, 2012, will remain current until they are next revised effective January 1, 2016. Readers should refer to the full text of the Rules in the official publications, *The Rules of Golf* and *The Decisions on the Rules of Golf*, which are published by the United States Golf Association and R&A Rules Limited.

This publication summarizes some of *The Rules of Golf* as interpreted by the author. The United States Golf Association does not warrant the accuracy of the author's interpretations.

The author thanks Layne Williams of the Georgia State Golf Association for his assistance on the book, Warren Grant for the interior photographs, Todd Sentell for serving as the golfer, and the Atlanta Athletic Club for permission to use its golf courses as the site.

This book is printed on acid-free paper.

*This book is for the staff of the Georgia State
Golf Association and their contributions
to the game of golf.*

Contents

PART 1 Getting Started

PART 2 Playing the Round

PART 3 Golf Rules and Course Strategy

viii

Foreword

Raymond Floyd

At the age of 20, I won the St. Petersburg Open in 1963. That was a great start to my career as a golf professional, and I eventually won the Masters, the PGA Championship, and the U.S. Open among my other PGA Tour victories. No matter how well I played, though, if I had made mistakes regarding the Rules I would not have won. As much as a shot hit into a water hazard or a topped tee shot, a lack of knowledge about the Rules can hurt a golfer's score. That was instilled in me at an early age, and it has remained important whenever I step onto a golf course.

Dishonesty is a rarity in golf. I think that I know the reason why. While there may be training aids to assist you when you practice, and anyone can benefit from good instruction and playing tips, once you're on the course you make each shot by yourself. Unless you are in a tournament, you are responsible only to yourself for following the Rules. Any golfer who takes the time and effort to learn the game, whatever that person's ability, wants to play the game as it should be played—and that means playing by the Rules.

Knowing the Rules well can also save a golfer strokes during a round. The strategic benefit of realizing your best option in any situation on a golf course may be the best reason for knowing the Rules well.

There is always room for improvement for anyone's golf swing. Knowing the Rules is another aspect of preparing for a round of golf. Knowing the Rules also contributes to a golfer's confidence during a round, and a good mental attitude should help a golfer make better shots. The more you know about golf the more you will enjoy every round, whether you are in contention in the final round of the Masters or trying to break 90 for the first time on your local course.

Raymond Floyd won 21 times on the PGA Tour. He played on seven Ryder Cup teams from 1969 through 1991, and he was the nonplaying captain of the 1989 U.S. team.

Foreword

Louise Suggs

I took to golf at an early age, being instructed first by my father, who himself was a good enough athlete to play professional baseball. I also had the good fortune to play with and watch Bob Jones play golf at what is now East Lake Golf Club, which in the late 1930s was the site of the Atlanta Athletic Club. He arranged for me to have playing privileges at the club. When I once asked Mr. Jones how hard I should hit the ball, he replied, "Hit the hell out of it; it'll come down somewhere."

I won the Georgia State Women's Amateur at age 16 in 1940, then repeated as champion two years later. I won the Southern Women's Amateur Championship in 1941 and the North and South Women's Amateur in 1942, when I was still not yet 18. At that time, prior to the formation of the Ladies Professional Golf Association, women's amateur golf attracted the best players in the game. Further evidence of how good the amateurs were is that Polly Riley, as an amateur, won the first official LPGA event in 1950, the Tampa Women's Open.

From my earliest days in competitive golf, I had to compete against and beat women with far more experience than myself. Knowing the Rules of the game and how to conduct myself on the golf course was as important as my golf swing in scoring well. If I made mistakes relevant to the Rules, penalty strokes would have spoiled my score. My father's influence was important in this area of the game, and knowing the Rules gave me the confidence I needed to compete at the highest levels of the game.

The Rules of Golf apply equally to anyone who plays the game, whether a 12-year-old junior or a 70-year-old senior golfer, whether male or female, and whether you are playing in Florida, Scotland, or New Zealand. To me this is one of the best aspects of golf. It is the same game for everyone. Every golfer has the same responsibility to know the Rules and even to call penalties on one's own play if the situation requires.

The most notorious Rules situations have often been inadvertent mistakes by players. One of these was at the 1957 U.S. Women's Open at Winged Foot. Jackie Pung finished the championship one stroke ahead of Betsy Rawls and thought that she had won. Shortly afterward, while being interviewed in the press room, she realized that she had signed a scorecard with an incorrect 5 for the fourth hole where she actually had a 6. Since she had signed an incorrect scorecard, that mistake cost her the championship, which was awarded to Rawls. What is most striking about any story of a breach of the Rules is just how rarely that has affected the outcome of a tournament. Golfers pride themselves on knowing the Rules.

I can't claim to have been an expert on the Rules when I played competitive golf, but I knew enough that I never suffered any problems during a tournament round. One reason for the early success of the LPGA, which I had a role in founding, was that spectators knew the game was being played by the highest standards and with a strict adherence to the Rules. Golf should be played that way today, and those who enjoy golf as much as I have for more than 75 years will understand why that is important. Reading this book will allow you to share in that appreciation for the Rules.

Louise Suggs is credited with winning 58 LPGA titles during her career as a professional golfer. When she won the U.S. Women's Open in 1949, her victory margin was 14 strokes, still an LPGA record. The LPGA recognizes the most accomplished first-year player on the LPGA Tour with the Louise Suggs Rolex Rookie of the Year Award. In 2007, the United States Golf Association presented Suggs the Bob Jones Award, given in recognition of distinguished sportsmanship in golf.

Introduction

Every four years the Rules of Golf undergo some revision. For 2012 there were several changes made to the Rules, as determined by the R&A and the United States Golf Association. A complete review of the principal changes for 2012 to the Rules can be found at http://www.usga.org/uploadedFiles/USGA Home/rules/rules_pg5-7_rules.pdf. In this third edition of *Golf Rules & Etiquette Simplified*, changes have been made to the text to reflect relevant changes to the Rules. Many of the changes made in the Rules were matters of clarification of the terms used to define a situation. This book is an introduction to the Rules of Golf and not an exhaustive account of the Rules; therefore, not every change is reflected in this third edition, especially those changes affecting amateur status. In updating this book the focus has been on changes in a penalty or how to proceed in a specific situation.

The emphasis of this guidebook is on what could be termed common Rules. For example, the particulars of match play are not discussed. The complete Rules are described in *The Rules of Golf* published by the United States Golf Association (USGA) and the R&A. A complete list of the Rules of Golf and the Decisions on the Rules of Golf can be found on the USGA website (http://www.usga.org/Rule-Books /Rules-of-Golf/Rule-01).

A Note on the Text

There are numerical references throughout this book to specific Rules that appear in the USGA's official publication, *The Rules of Golf*. Because the intention of this book is to simplify these Rules and make them more accessible to the beginning golfer, please refer to that publication if you seek a fuller explanation of any Rule outlined in the pages that follow.

GOLF RULES & ETIQUETTE SIMPLIFIED

Getting
Started

Golf Clubs

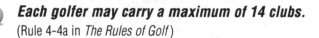

Each golfer may carry a maximum of 14 clubs.
(Rule 4-4a in _The Rules of Golf_)

Breaches of the Rules on a municipal course on a Saturday afternoon in July usually do not receive recognition through worldwide coverage. When a Rules incident occurs in a major championship everyone knows about it, especially if the incident affects the outcome of who wins. In the final round of the 2001 British Open Ian Woosnam and his caddie made a mistake that contributed to his not winning. Woosnam had been practicing before the round with two drivers trying to determine which one he would use for the day. When he finished with driving practice he went to the chipping and putting practice area and continued there. Then he and his caddie hurried to the first tee. Unfortunately, neither Woosnam nor his caddie counted the number of clubs in his bag upon arrival at the first tee. The first hole was a par 3, and Woosnam put his tee shot

A player may carry only 14 clubs in the bag, but the set can be made up of any combination of clubs. The set shown here includes 4- through 9-irons, a pitching wedge, a sand wedge, a lob wedge, a putter, a 3-hybrid (equivalent of a 3-iron), a driver, a 3-wood, and a 5-wood. An alternative set could contain 2- through 9-irons, putter, a pitching wedge, a sand wedge, a driver, 4-wood and a 3-wood. It is up to each golfer which clubs will be the best implements to play the game.

within less than a foot of the hole. He birdied the hole and proceeded to the next tee. That was when his caddie, when pulling the driver from the bag, realized that he was still carrying both drivers and therefore had 15 clubs in his bag. Woosnam received a two-stroke penalty for the mistake. He made bogey in two out of the next three holes. Woosnam finished the British Open four shots behind the winner, David Duval.

If you discover that you have more than 14 clubs in your bag, remove the extra clubs before the round.

If you start a round and then discover that you have too many clubs, you must declare the additional clubs to be out of play. (Rule 4-4c)

One way of ensuring that the club will remain identified as unplayable during the round is to insert it upside down in the golf bag so that the handle protrudes from the bag and the clubhead is at the bottom of the bag. That is not a necessity that is part of the Rules, but it will prevent the club from being used inadvertently. What is necessary if a player discovers that there are too many clubs in the bag is to announce to other players that the club or clubs are not in play for the stipulated round.

5

● *There is no official set of 14 clubs. A golfer may carry a putter, 3- through 9-irons (seven clubs), pitching wedge, sand wedge, lob wedge, and three woods. Another variation might be putter, 1- through 9-irons (nine clubs), pitching wedge, sand wedge, putter, and two woods. The selection of clubs is up to the player, including carrying two putters if that seems productive, 5- through 9-irons (five clubs), sand wedge, and six woods (driver, 3-wood, 4-wood, 5-wood, 7-wood, and 9-wood).*

● *A player may not alter the playing characteristics of a club through a round, such as adding lead tape to the back of a clubhead.* (Rule 4-2a)

Changing the characteristics of a club is not restricted to cosmetic changes. If a player is twirling a club to pass the time prior to teeing off on the third hole and the club lands on the golf cart and the shaft is broken, that would be considered to be done outside the normal course of play. That is not allowed. When a club is damaged during a round, other than in the normal course of play, then the club must be removed from play from that stipulated round.

Nothing can be applied to the face of a club to affect the movement of the ball. (Rule 4-2b)

In the 1930s some professional golfers applied substances such as Vaseline to the surface of their driver to achieve less spin on the ball coming off the clubface. In the current era, with the golf ball contributing so much to length, players have technology on their side and tricks aren't necessary to achieve unusual effects for the flight of the golf ball.

> Byron Nelson used the same putter to win 8 PGA Tour events in 1944, 18 in 1945, and then 6 during 1946 before retiring at the end of that year from the Tour.

If a club is damaged during the normal course of play a golfer has three options:

- **Use the damaged club as is for that stipulated round.**
- **Repair the club during the round without delaying play.**
- **Replace the club without undue delay of the round.** (Rule 4-3a)

If a player damages a club intentionally (bending the shaft, breaking off the clubhead, etc.), then that club may not be used through the remainder of the round.

Byron Nelson used the same putter to win 8 PGA Tour events in 1944, 18 in 1945, and then 6 during 1946 before retiring at the end of that year from the Tour. His friend and four-ball partner on Tour, Harold "Jug" McSpaden, witnessed Nelson make this remarkable string of victories. In fact, McSpaden set a record for most second-place finishes in a calendar year on Tour in 1945 with 13. After Nelson announced his retirement he put away his golf clubs and spent his time tending to his ranch in Roanoke, Texas, 20 miles northeast of Fort Worth. Thinking that Nelson no longer needed his magical putter, McSpaden asked to borrow it. Unlike the even-tempered Nelson, McSpaden could become upset on the golf course when things didn't go his way. Though warned by Nelson not to damage his favorite putter, McSpaden in a fit of anger broke off the head of the club. Nelson couldn't get too mad at him, though. McSpaden had named his son Byron after him.

Golf Balls

Nothing shall be done to alter the surface character of a ball to change its playing characteristics.

Players should mark their ball prior to a round so that easy identification of the ball is possible while on the golf course.

Marking a golf ball prior to a round becomes important if a ball must be identified in a situation that could result in a more severe penalty if the ball cannot be identified. An example would be if a golf ball became lodged in a portion of a tree that is not reachable by the golfer in order to make a shot. If the golfer cannot confirm that the ball is his or hers by pointing out the identifying marks, then the ball is determined to be lost.

If as a result of a stroke a ball comes apart, then the stroke is canceled and a player must replace that ball without penalty.

Mud that collects on a ball after a shot anywhere on the course other than the putting green cannot be removed. On the green, the ball may be cleaned, though the player must place a ball marker by the ball prior to lifting the ball.

On the Driving Range

 Silence cell phones while on the driving range.

Cell phones have become omnipresent. However important it is to receive certain phone calls, since it cannot be predicted when the phone might ring, it is unfair to other golfers to insist that they tolerate a disruption to their golf swing, even on the practice tee. The disruption of a cell phone's ring may seem minor, unless you have downloaded the ring tone to Jimi Hendrix's "Manic Depression" to alert you when you have a call. Even worse is someone discussing plans for a movie after the round for 15 minutes while everyone else on the practice tee must listen to one end of the conversation. Other golfers are due no disruptions in their round. The world functioned well enough prior to the era of cell phones, and you can function without yours for four hours.

Do not stand too close to other players.

> The disruption of a cell phone's ring may seem minor, unless you have downloaded the ring tone to Jimi Hendrix's "Manic Depression" to alert you when you have a call.

Although some practice tees may have a row of talented golfers who would not swing a club wildly nor do something else foolish, accidents do happen. A clubhead can break off during a swing, or a ball can be hit sideways into other players.

Do not walk in front of the teeing area to retrieve a ball or tee.

Playing the Round

Etiquette

The spirit of the game is to be respectful of other players' safety as well as their enjoyment of the game without risk of harm or disruption due to fits of anger over bad shots, the weather, errant bounces of the ball, or other misfortunes.

Here's a trick question about the Rules: if a golf course has a foursome on every hole, how many rules officials are present? The answer is 72. Four golfers per hole times 18 holes equals 72 rules officials. Every person who is playing on a golf course should comply with the Rules. That has always been a part of the game of golf, and it will remain part of the game as long as it is played. Not only should a golfer respect the Rules, but the other players should be able to play the game without the distraction of one golfer berating himself or herself over the vicissitudes of cruel fate, equipment failure, or design flaws in the golf course that resulted in a score of 20 over par.

As Byron Nelson once said, "Good golf is easy; bad golf is hard." Certainly bad golf is hard to accept sometimes. Despite that, golf should be congenial at all times.

A player's response to the misfortunes of a bad swing or a bad bounce on the golf course may be frustration at times. As Byron Nelson once said, "Good golf is easy; bad golf is hard." Certainly bad golf is hard to accept sometimes. Despite that, golf should be congenial at all times.

Arrive at the first tee ready to play 10 minutes before your tee time.

Any golf course that gets a lot of play, especially on weekends, has players that want to get on the course, but may be waiting to see if a group does not show up or is late. Be careful at your course because if you do not show up 10 minutes prior to your tee time the course may give another group the time.

Be aware of the position of other players before swinging a club for practice or a golf shot.

The importance of caution on a golf course cannot be overstated. A golf ball flying through the air at over 80 miles an hour can cause serious injury.

Yelling "fore" to announce errant shots is an obligation, not just a point of courtesy. Even a practice swing can do damage to a person who is hit in the eye or in the teeth. Look before you swing, and then pay attention to where the ball is going and if any other golfer may be in the ball's flight path. Any harm done by a golfer on a golf course is usually the liability of the golfer who creates the damage, not the golf course. That would include breaking a pane of glass on a house or cracking a car windshield.

Allow players in the group ahead on the golf course to get out of range of any shot before hitting.

There is no benefit to running a ball up to a group ahead of your group. It is easy on a golf course to misjudge distance or to hit the shot of your life and get 30 more yards' carry from a particular shot. Worse than running the ball to within 10 yards of the players in the group ahead would be to hit the ball among them. That is dangerous and not just a nuisance. Allow players ahead to leave a green or to advance to their next shot on the fairway before hitting your shot. A crowded course sometimes creates frustrations when the pace of play is slow, but nothing is gained by taking the risk of hurting other players.

● **Announce to workers on the course if a shot may possibly endanger them.**

● **Use the term "fore" to announce that a ball may be coming close to another player or group.**

● **Any movement, jangling of pocket change, conversation, or other noise is a distraction to someone about to make a shot. Remain silent and still while others are hitting.**

There is a scene near the beginning of the movie *Bringing Up Baby*, starring Cary Grant and Katharine Hepburn, that illustrates this point. Grant is playing golf with a man who he thinks is a potential donor to the museum where Grant works. Through the round Grant is making his case while his playing partner is trying to play golf. Finally, he stops Grant and tells him that on a golf course he only talks about golf. Beyond trying to talk directly to someone trying to hit a shot, it is also important to notice whether talking to another member of the group will disturb a player trying to hit a shot.

● **Keep a good distance away from a golfer about to hit a shot, and stand to the side of a golfer, not behind.**

● *Silence cell phones while on a golf course.*

● *Maintain a pace of play that allows your group to play as soon as the group ahead is out of range.*

● *If due to slow play a space of one hole opens between the group ahead and your group, invite the group playing behind to play through.*

There is no shame in having to search for a lost ball or having someone in your group take four shots to reach the green on a par-3 hole. There is shame in requiring a group behind you that plays at a faster pace to endure repeated delays due to poor play through an entire round. You are not only holding up play for the group immediately behind; you are holding up play for the entire golf course and everyone on it. Allow faster groups to play through. The usual procedure for alerting the group following to play through is to leave the fairway open for the next group's shots and then wave them ahead. Make sure to leave ample room for any errant shots they might hit. Do not stand on the edge of the green on a par-3 hole and expect even the best golfers to put their shots close to the flag and therefore not bring your group into harm's way. Playing through another group sometimes makes even competent golfers nervous, and a bad shot is the result. Watch

19

the shots as the golfers advance, and don't be so lost in conversation that a ball could hit you in the head.

 Consider your next shot's distance and the appropriate club before it is your turn to hit, then have the club in hand and be ready to hit the shot when it is your turn.

It is always good to know where your fellow competitors are on the golf course and when each person is about to hit. It is possible to do that and at the same time prepare for your shot by identifying the yardage for the next shot, where you want to hit the ball to your best advantage, and which club will serve that purpose. Do not wait until the person who hits before you makes a shot to begin the process of determining which club you will hit. Another element of this is the practice swing—that's one swing, not four. Nor should a divot be made when taking a practice swing.

> Do not wait until the person who hits before you makes a shot to begin the process of determining which club you will hit.

 In a sand bunker, after playing your stroke, cover any hole created by a shot, rake the sand smooth

of footprints made while in the bunker, and replace the rake to a position outside the bunker.

Repair all divot holes on the green created by the impact of a ball upon landing.

In taking a practice swing, do not make a divot with the club.

The principle of leaving the golf course as you would like to find it is critical in golf. Leaving footprints in a bunker is not just a matter of housekeeping on the course. The next player who lands in an unraked bunker may have to play out of a footprint if the bunker is not raked smooth after a player enters it. Other players who leave a bunker unraked are creating poor conditions for you.

Repairing ball marks is another instance of the principle of leaving the golf course as you would like to find it. The right way to repair a divot is to use a divot repair tool around the edges of the divot to push the grass back over the divot hole, then smooth the area with the clubhead of a putter.

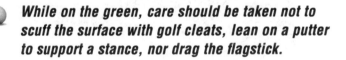

While on the green, care should be taken not to scuff the surface with golf cleats, lean on a putter to support a stance, nor drag the flagstick.

One of the biggest advances in golf course conditioning in the past 10 years is the transition to soft spikes. Metal spikes easily tore up the green surface if golfers did not pick up their feet. The area immediately around the hole got the worst damage because that was where most of the foot traffic occurred on the putting green. Casual damage to the green surface can also come from placing one's weight on the putter while using it for balance.

When the flagstick is pulled from the hole and placed out of range, it should be laid on the ground, not dropped.

● *After putting, replace the flagstick properly before leaving the green so that it is standing upright.*

● *Entering a score on the scorecard should be done upon arrival at the next teeing ground, not while standing on the green where play just finished.*

On the
Teeing Ground

You may choose which set of tees you will hit from.

The New Zealand golf professional John Lister, who played on the U.S. PGA Tour for several years, was once asked by an amateur which tees to choose when playing a round. Lister, noting that on that golf course there were white tees, blue tees, and yellow tees, said, "Start at the white tees. When you can shoot par from there, move back to the next set. If you can manage to shoot par from that set, move back again. If you can shoot par from the back tees, start entering competitions." Many contemporary golf courses on the tee shot require long carries over water hazards, marshes, waste areas, or other hazards that only the best golfers can hit beyond.

> Play from tees that allow you to enjoy the game. Any good score, whichever set of tees is used, is more enjoyable, and a source of pride, than a bad score from inappropriate tees.

There is little fun to be had in playing from a set of tees that doesn't allow a golfer to score well on almost any hole. Play from tees that allow you to enjoy the game. Any good score, whichever set of tees is used, is more enjoyable, and a source of pride, than a bad score from inappropriate tees.

Position a golf bag away from the teeing ground.

If you are carrying a golf bag on the course, position the golf bag off the surface of the teeing ground. Doing this not only protects the surface of the tee box, but the golf bag then does not become a distraction to anyone hitting a tee shot.

The order of play is determined by the players in a group, with the low scorer on each hole considered to have the honor on the next hole, that is, the privilege of hitting first. The next lowest scorer would hit next, and so on. (Rule 10-2a)

While it is good to follow some protocol for identifying who will drive first, for the sake of play it sometimes makes sense to allow the first person prepared to hit to go ahead and hit.

The teeing ground is a box determined by the line between the front edge of two tee markers and their outside limits, two club lengths directly behind the front of each tee marker and perpendicular to them, and a line parallel to the line between the front edge of the tee markers.

The player may stand outside the teeing ground in order to hit the drive, as long as the ball is within the teeing ground. (Rule 11-1)

If a ball accidentally rolls off the tee it may be replaced without penalty. (Rule 11-3)

● **The tee markers may not be repositioned, unless on the second shot when they become an obstruction.** (Rule 11-2)

● **Stand away and to the side of the golfer teeing off, not directly behind the person.**

If a golfer hits a tee shot that comes to rest behind a tee marker, that tee marker becomes a man-made obstruction that can be moved for the purpose of the next shot. It should be replaced in its previous position after the shot.

6

Through the Green

● *Play the ball as it lies.*

● *The player farthest from the hole hits first.*

● *If a ball at rest is moved by the player there is a one-stroke penalty, and the ball must be returned to its original position.*

One of the most famous Rules incidents in the history of the game involved this Rule. Bobby Jones was playing in the first round of the 1925 U.S. Open at Worcester Country Club in Massachusetts. On the eleventh hole his approach shot fell short of the green and dropped into the high grass that was typical of Open course setups even in that era. Jones prepared to make his next shot. When his clubhead

A golfer is not allowed to improve the lie of the ball no matter where the ball is on the golf course. The exception to the Rule comes when a golfer may be endangered by an outside agency on the golf course such as bees, an alligator, or snakes.

swept the grass, Jones saw his ball move. Jones told Walter Hagan, who was playing with him, and a USGA rules official that a Rules infraction had occurred and that he would assess himself the one-stroke penalty appropriate for the infraction. The response at the time by those watching the competition, whether spectators or rules officials, was that

Jones was wrong because no one had seen the ball move, and Bobby Jones drew the largest crowd of fans. When he turned in his scorecard he confirmed that he had taken the penalty stroke. When later praised for his adherence to the Rules he replied, "You might as well praise a man for not robbing a bank." When the tournament ended Jones was tied with Willie Macfarlane. Had he not given himself the penalty shot he would have won the event at the end of regulation play. He and Macfarlane went on to tie in the first playoff round, and then Jones lost by a stroke in the second playoff round.

- *Be prepared to hit your shot when it is your turn to play.*

- *You are not allowed to clean mud from the ball lying on the fairway or in the rough.*

- *A ball embedded in the ground in its own pitch mark in a closely mown area can be marked, removed, and dropped.*

- *Before hitting any shot, note the proximity of other golfers, including in the group ahead. Be prepared to alert other golfers about any errant shot.*

A ball embedded in the ground in a closely mown area can be marked for its position, cleaned, and dropped at a point close to the ball's original position. The reason a ball would become embedded in the ground is that the ground would be so soggy that the ball penetrates the surface. That would be considered an embedded ball; thus, a player is allowed relief.

After five minutes of searching, the ball is lost. (Definition of "Lost Ball")

After you have addressed your ball, if you cause the ball to move, it must be returned to its original position and one penalty stroke is incurred. If the ball moves and it is known or virtually certain that the golfer did not cause the ball to move—for

example, the wind caused the ball to move—then no penalty is incurred and the ball is played from its new position. (Rule 18-2b)

If a player grounds the club either immediately in front of or immediately behind the ball, it is considered addressed, whether the golfer has taken a stance or not (see definitions in the Rules of Golf). Jack Nicklaus throughout his career has always kept the clubhead off the ground when he takes his stance. That way, if the ball moves, he has not compounded the situation by having grounded the clubhead and therefore addressed the ball.

> Jack Nicklaus throughout his career has always kept the clubhead off the ground when he takes his stance. That way, if the ball moves, he has not compounded the situation by having grounded the clubhead and therefore addressed the ball.

Allow faster groups to play through, including if searching for a ball holds up play.

Do not take a divot from the fairway on a practice swing.

33

Position equipment (golf bag, golf cart) out of the line of play of all golfers.

A shot that strikes a player's own equipment results in a one-stroke penalty, so it is not only a matter of courtesy to get equipment out of the line of play, but part of the game. Equipment includes a golf bag or the player's own golf cart.

Do not alter the golf course, such as breaking a tree limb, in order to facilitate a shot.

Often a ball comes to rest near foliage or tree limbs that if removed might allow a golfer an easier opportunity to hit the shot. Since a golfer is to leave the course as it is found, breaking off a tree limb, stamping down the grass behind a ball, or other ways of changing the golf course in order to hit a shot are prohibited.

Players may ask other players for information about distance but must not ask for advice, such as information about the club another player used to make a shot or how to play a specific shot. (Rule 8-1)

A ball can be declared unplayable at any time and anywhere on the course, except in water hazards. Three options are available once the ball is declared unplayable (all three options incur one penalty stroke):

- *The player may drop the ball within two club lengths, no closer to the hole, from the original position of the ball.*
- *The player may drop the ball on a line extending backward from the hole through where the ball lay.*
- *The player may drop the ball at the point of the last stroke.* (Rule 28)

If in dropping the ball, the ball rolls to another undesirable position, the player must play the ball as it lies or declare it unplayable.

A golf ball may come to rest in the fork of tree limbs or in between tree roots. A golfer has the option in such circumstances of taking a drop within two club lengths of the original position of the ball to gain relief from the situation. One penalty stroke is added to the player's score. It is at the golfer's discretion to deem that a ball is unplayable.

Another example of a potentially unplayable lie

A ball that lands on the wrong putting green must be removed and cannot be played from that putting green. There is no penalty stroke. The ball shall be dropped within one club length of the nearest point of relief no nearer the hole from the putting green surface. (Rule 25-3)

A ball struck twice in the act of the hitting the ball results in one penalty stroke. (Rule 14-4)

A player who discovers that a wrong ball has been hit must return to where the ball was hit to play the correct ball. Two penalty strokes are incurred, but the strokes made with the wrong ball do not count. If the correct ball cannot be located, then a new ball must be dropped at the point of the last stroke. One penalty stroke is added to the score with the drop. (Rule 15-3)

If an outside agency (animal, bird, spectator) is struck by a shot, there is no penalty. The ball must be played as it lies. (Rule 19-1)

A loose impediment such as a twig or stone can be removed.

If a twig, leaf, rock, or other loose impediment comes to rest on the ball, the item may be removed to allow the golfer to hit the ball.

Another example of a loose impediment that can be removed before hitting a shot

 If an outside agency moves a player's ball (for example, a bird picks up a ball and later drops the ball at another position), the ball must be returned to its original position. If an outside agency removes a ball that then cannot be found, a new

ball is substituted at the point where the original ball was removed. However, the golfer must be certain that an outside agency moved the ball. (Rule 18-1)

When a ball struck from the teeing ground, the fairway, a bunker, or a hazard hits another ball there is no penalty stroke. The ball that was moved is replaced to its original position. However, if both balls were on the putting green and a putted ball strikes another ball, two penalty strokes are incurred by the player who made the putt. (Rules 18-5 and 19-5a)

No relief is allowed for a ball that comes to rest in a divot made by another player, or ground without grass.

The 1998 U.S. Open at Olympic raised the issue of whether it is fair to golfers to have to play out of divots. Repair of divots on the course included spreading sand in each divot. On several holes, because of the slope of a fairway, the balls gathered in approximately the same area on the fairway, with the result that after two days of play many golfers were hitting approach shots out of divots. There is no relief from these situations, and the Rule is still to play the ball as it lies.

41

A ball coming to rest in a divot made by another player is an unfortunate situation, but no relief is allowed.

If the ball when hit strikes you or your equipment, which can include a golf bag or electric cart, then one penalty stroke is incurred. (Rule 19-2)

If a ball cannot be found after a search of five minutes, then the ball is lost. Through the green the next shot is from the position of the last shot after a drop, or the ball may be hit from a tee if the last shot was from the teeing ground. (Rule 27-1c)

A ball is deemed lost because of certain actions. However, if the ball is lost, there are exceptions from the usual result of having to hit another shot from the position previously played. These exceptions include:

- *The ball cannot be found in an obstruction.*
- *The ball cannot be found in an abnormal ground condition.*
- *The ball is in a water hazard.*
- *The ball has been moved by an outside agency.*

In the exceptions listed above, if the player has knowledge or virtual certainty that the ball is located in each condition, he may proceed under the applicable Rule in each circumstance. For example, the options available other than stroke and distance apply if the ball is lost in a water hazard.

43

Within the golf course (not out of bounds), if a ball comes to rest in a position that interferes (due to an immovable obstruction) with a golfer's ability to swing a club or advance the ball, then relief can be obtained by a free drop within one club length of the nearest point of relief and no nearer the hole.

If a ball cannot be hit due to an immovable obstruction such as a sprinkler system box, then a free drop is allowed no closer to the hole at the nearest point where relief is available.

If a ball is suspected to be lost outside a water hazard after a shot, then a player should play a

provisional ball. The player must announce that the new ball is a provisional and then drop the ball at the point where the first shot was hit. If the last position was the teeing ground, then the player can tee up the ball again. The player must play the provisional ball prior to looking for a lost ball. (Rule 27-2a)

A ball coming to rest on a sprinkler head can be moved. A player is not required to stand on a sprinkler head to make a shot.

Relief is allowed from immovable obstructions such as paved roads or cart paths. (Rule 24-2)

If a ball is dropped with the following results, it must be dropped again if it rolls:

- *Into a hazard*
- *Out of a hazard*
- *Onto a putting green*
- *Out of bounds*
- *Into a position that does not allow complete relief from an obstruction, abnormal ground condition, or the wrong putting green*
- *Farther than two club lengths away from where the ball struck the course*
- *Nearer to the hole*
- *Onto the player or equipment* (Rule 20-2)

45

A ball that comes to rest on a sprinkler head can be moved. This would also apply to a water drain grate or a pump house for a lake, both of which are deemed immovable obstructions (as opposed to movable obstructions). Relief is a free drop within one club length of the nearest point of relief, but no nearer the hole.

Relief is also allowed if the normal swing path of the club would damage it by contact with the sprinkler head.

If a ball is not resting on the sprinkler head but the player's stance to reach the ball requires standing on a sprinkler head, then relief is available.

No relief is allowed if the ball is not on the sprinkler head and the player does not have to stand on the sprinkler head.

If a ball comes to rest on a paved road or a cart path, relief is allowed because these conditions are considered immovable obstructions. A golfer should first take a stance at the nearest point of relief, then has the opportunity to drop the ball one club length from that point, but no nearer the hole. The nearest point of relief would be where interference would cease to exist. Interference includes stance, lie of ball, and area of intended swing.

Out of Bounds

- *Out of bounds is an area defined as not part of the golf course, usually defined by white stakes. Local rules may specify certain areas as out of bounds that are not marked, such as a road or parking lot.*

- *A ball resting in bounds may be hit by a player whose stance is out of bounds.*

- *A ball resting along the out-of-bounds line is not considered out of bounds unless the entire ball is resting out of bounds. If the ball is touching the golf course, then it is considered to be in bounds.*

- *If a shot is perceived to be out of bounds, play a provisional ball from the same point prior to searching for the ball out of bounds. If the first ball is determined to be out of bounds one penalty stroke is added.* (Rule 27-1b)

White stakes are one way to identify the out of bounds on a golf course. Out of bounds can be along the side of a fairway, behind a green, or any other area so identified, such as a parking lot, swimming pool, or road. If a player's ball comes to rest in bounds but an out-of-bounds stake impedes a swing or the flight of a ball, the stake cannot be moved for the convenience of the golfer.

54

A ball that is resting in bounds may be hit by a golfer whose stance is in the area out of bounds.

The line created between the inside edge of two out-of-bounds stakes at ground level defines the margin of the out-of-bounds area. A ball resting along that line is not considered out of bounds because a portion of the ball is touching the golf course.

In a Bunker

- **A ball is deemed in a bunker if any part of the ball touches the bunker.**

- **The club cannot touch the sand prior to a stroke. If it does, this is considered testing the sand, which results in two penalty strokes.** (Rule 13-4a)

The principle of playing the ball as it lies applies to sand bunkers as it does all other areas of the golf course.

A player may not test the character of the sand in a bunker by touching the sand with the club prior to a shot. Whether the sand is wet or dry, dense or thin must be discovered when the shot is made. Therefore, a golfer should be careful in taking a stance in a bunker not to ground the club—that is, bring the clubhead to rest in the sand behind the ball as might be done on a fairway without penalty.

If a golfer might strike another player's ball lying in a bunker, then that second ball can be marked. The exact lie the ball had prior to being marked should be duplicated when the ball is replaced, including if it was buried in the sand.

- **When two balls are in close proximity in a bunker, one ball can be marked, for example with a tee, then replaced after the first ball is hit.** (Rules 22-2 and 20-3b(iii))

- **Loose impediments in a bunker must not be removed or touched (twigs, leaves, stones). Some courses have local rules allowing removal of stones from a sand bunker.** (Rule 13-4c)

Unlike the relief allowed through the green, where a golfer can remove loose impediments, in a bunker that relief is not allowed. Local rules at a golf course may allow the removal of stones or rocks because these create a risk to the safety of the golfers playing the hole.

IN A BUNKER

If a rake in a bunker obstructs a shot, then the rake may be removed. If the ball moves during this process, it may be replaced without penalty.

A rake in a bunker is considered a man-made object, and therefore it can be removed from the swing path of the golfer.

Relief cannot be obtained for conditions such as a footprint in a bunker.

At the twelfth hole at Augusta National during the 2003 Masters a player hit a tee shot that went into the bunker behind the green. The ball landed in a footprint left by a caddie from the previous group when exiting the bunker. However unfortunate the bad lie was for the player, he had to play from the lie that he encountered in the bunker. He was not allowed any relief.

At the twelfth hole at Augusta National during the 2003 Masters a player hit a tee shot that went into the bunker behind the green. The ball landed in a footprint left by a caddie from the previous group when exiting the bunker. However unfortunate the bad lie was for the player, he had to play from the lie that he encountered in the bunker. He was not allowed any relief.

A practice swing is allowed in a bunker as long as the club does not touch the sand.

If a bunker contains abnormal ground conditions (casual water, ground under repair), and the player's stance would have to be within that area, then the player can take relief. The

If a ball comes to rest in a footprint of another golfer, the hoofprint of a deer, or the pawprint of a dog, there is no relief from this condition.

player may drop the ball in the bunker away from the abnormal ground condition, no more than one club length from the nearest point of relief from the abnormal ground condition.

Although grounding the club in a bunker, or touching the sand with the club prior to a shot, is not allowed, a golfer can take a practice swing in a bunker, being careful not to touch the sand with any part of the club or move the ball in the process.

A ball in a bunker that is in an unplayable lie, such as buried between the grass lip and the sand, can be dropped with one penalty stroke added. The options for the drop:

- *Drop the ball in the bunker within two club lengths of the original position, but no closer to the hole.*
- *Drop the ball in the bunker on a line from the hole extending through the original point of the ball.*
- *Drop at the position of the last stroke.*

It is permissible for a player to smooth sand or soil in a hazard at any time, as long as the player is not improving the lie of the ball, his stance or swing, his line of play, or the area where he is dropping or placing his ball and the smoothing is for the sole purpose of caring for the course.

In a Water Hazard

If a ball touches the boundary of a water hazard, defined as its margin, it is deemed to be in the hazard.

In the circumstance of out of bounds, the ball must be entirely outside the out-of-bounds line to be considered out of bounds. With a water hazard, if the ball is touching the margin of the water hazard, then it is considered to be in the hazard and all Rules applicable to water hazards are in force.

There are two types of water hazards:

- *Water hazards, marked by yellow stakes and/or lines*
- *Lateral water hazards, marked by red stakes and/or lines* (Rule 26-1)

If a ball enters a water hazard a player has the following options, the first being to play the ball as it lies, without grounding the club prior to hitting a shot. The other options require one penalty stroke added:

- *Drop the ball behind the water hazard on a line extending from the hole through the point where the ball last crossed the water hazard margin.*
- *Drop the ball at the point of the last shot.*

One option for relief from a regular water hazard (marked by yellow stakes) or a lateral water hazard (marked by red stakes) is along a line from the hole through the point where the ball last crossed the margin of the hazard. The golfer may drop at any point along this line, however far back the player chooses.

The correct method of dropping the ball

If a ball goes into a regular water hazard or lateral water hazard, one option is to drop a ball at the point of the original shot and hit from there.

Incorrect methods of dropping the ball

If a ball enters a lateral water hazard a player has the aforementioned options, plus two others:

- *Drop the ball within two club lengths of the point where the ball last crossed the margin of the hazard, no nearer the hole.*
- *Drop the ball within two club lengths of a point on the opposite margin of the hazard that is equidistant from the hole from where the ball last crossed the margin of the lateral hazard (a creek, for example), but no closer to the hole.*

The stakes defining a water hazard may be removed if they obstruct a player's shot.

A local rule may provide a drop zone near a water hazard as an additional place for a player to drop the ball for the next shot after hitting into a water hazard.

Many golf courses provide drop zones forward of the regular set of teeing grounds in order to move play along. If there is a long carry over water or other hazard from the teeing ground to the putting green, then repeated attempts to cross that area may be futile—thus, the drop zone.

A player may lift a ball in a water hazard if he thinks it is his and he must lift the ball in order to identify it. The ball must be returned to its original position.

One option for relief from a ball that enters a lateral water hazard is to take a drop within two club lengths of the point where the ball last crossed the margin of the hazard. An easy way to determine the two-club-lengths' distance is to first lay a club down with one end at the point the ball last crossed the lateral hazard line, then flip the club to establish the point where the ball can be dropped. See the photos on the following page.

73

PLAYING THE ROUND

On the Putting Green

- *A ball is identified as being on the putting green if it is touching part of the putting green surface.*

- *The player whose ball lies farthest from the hole always putts first.* (Rule 10-2b)

- *Position equipment away from the putting green surface.*

- *A player may mark the ball's position on the putting green so that it is not in the line of play of other players. Once the ball is properly marked, it may be cleaned.* (Rules 16-1b and 20-1)

- *If a practice stroke accidentally moves the ball, then the ball must be replaced to its original position and one penalty stroke is incurred.*

A golf bag is sufficiently heavy to damage the surface of a putting green if it is placed there. Positioning a golf bag away from the putting green surface will protect the putting green. Care should also be taken to position the golf bag out of the line of other golfers who have yet to reach the putting green.

When a ball is marked on a putting green the marker should be placed as close to the position of the ball as possible. Even if a ball on the putting green is not in the immediate line of the putt of another golfer, a ball should be marked on the putting green as a point of courtesy so that no ball distracts any player who is putting.

ON THE PUTTING GREEN

A ball can be moved away from its original position and marked to prevent interference with another player's putt. The ball must be returned to its original position.

PLAYING THE ROUND

If the ball is embedded in the putting green surface a player is allowed to mark the ball, lift it, repair the pitch mark, and replace the ball in its original position.

On the putting green loose impediments such as twigs and stones may be removed without penalty. (Rule 23-1)

The following Rule is really a matter of through the green on the golf course because it is not on the putting green. However, because it affects the act of putting it is placed here among other considerations of what to do around and on the putting green.

If a sprinkler head interferes with a player's line of play (when the ball is resting off the putting green), then the ball cannot be moved. The ball may be moved to the nearest point of relief under the following circumstances:

- *The ball is lying on a sprinkler head.*
- *The player's stance requires standing on a sprinkler head.* (Rule 24-2a)

A local rule may be in effect allowing a player to be due relief from immovable obstructions within two club lengths of the green. The most typical such immovable obstruction close to a green would be a sprinkler head. If the ball is lying on the sprinkler head, that is considered an immovable obstruction and the ball can be dropped no nearer to the hole. The sprinkler head must be within two club lengths of the putting green, and the ball must be within two club lengths of the sprinkler head. The U.S. Open played at Pinehurst 2 had this local rule in effect, but it doesn't apply to every golf course.

If a ball when putted on the putting green strikes another ball at rest, then the ball that is struck must be returned to its original position. The person putting incurs a two-stroke penalty. (Rules 18-5 and 19-5a)

If a ball played from the putting green strikes the flagstick, whether being attended by another player or lying on the ground or the person attending the flagstick, then a two-stroke penalty is incurred. Any shot from off the green that hits the flagstick in the hole, unattended, does not incur a penalty. (Rule 17-3a)

In the 1939 U.S. Open Byron Nelson hit the flagstick six times during six rounds of golf, including holing out from the fairway on a shot with a 2-iron. The championship required six rounds because there were two playoff rounds before Nelson won. He used six different clubs in making these shots that hit the flagstick. Since all the shots were from off the green he did not incur any penalty strokes. In that era the flagstick was usually an inch in diameter and made out of wood. Today's flagsticks are made out of fiberglass or another flexible material and they are less than a half-inch thick.

When attending the flagstick as a courtesy to allow another golfer to see where the hole is located, the person attending the flagstick must be careful to pull the flagstick from the hole before the ball goes into the hole.

When a ball comes to rest between the side of the hole and the flagstick, the flagstick may be removed in such a way as to allow the ball to fall into the hole, completing the last stroke. (Rule 17-4)

A period of 10 seconds is allowed after the player has reached the hole to wait for a ball to drop that rests on the edge of the hole. (Rule 16-2)

A player is allowed only 10 seconds after reaching the hole to see if a ball resting on the edge of the hole falls into it. A player cannot in any way influence whether the ball goes into the hole such as by jumping up and down.

Golf Rules
and Course
Strategy

Knowing the Rules Can Improve Your Score

Most discussions of course strategy relate to where or how to play a certain shot on a particular hole to best ensure that the lowest possible score can be made. Course strategy involves laying up to avoid a hazard, or leaving an approach shot on the low side of the hole to allow an uphill putt, or using a putter to hit onto a putting green from 10 yards off to avoid the potential of sculling a wedge shot. It is always important in golf to realize that there is not just one way of playing a hole, and each golfer should decide what will work best. As is said, there are no diagrams on the scorecard, only the number of strokes taken from teeing ground until the final putt drops into the hole. There are always options.

The Rules are sometimes perceived as only a punitive element of golf, not relevant to how to best assure a low score. Since even the best players make bad swings occasionally and must deal with the consequences of hitting a ball into a water hazard, a sand bunker, or into an unplayable lie, it is always worthwhile for a golfer to be aware at all times about the options available for relief in a bad situation on the golf course.

One illustration about how a golfer can use an option when dealing with a lateral water hazard is the thirteenth hole at Augusta National during the playing of the Masters every year. The hole is a par 5 that plays as a dogleg left. The drive is uphill. After the fairway turns left it has a strong slope from the uphill portion on the right down to a creek that runs along the left side. Although the hole has been lengthened in recent years, it has always been a high risk/reward hole during the tournament. A well-placed drive that goes high on the fairway, possibly even making the turn left and rolling forward, can allow a second shot to the green for a possible eagle if the ball stays on the green and a player can make the putt. The risk involves the creek on the left side of the fairway. If a player on the drive tries to cut the corner too closely, then the tall trees lining the creek can come into play. A ball that hits the trees frequently falls back into Rae's Creek, a water hazard. Because the hole is a dogleg left, the best option is not to take relief two club lengths from the margin of the lateral water hazard but rather to go back along a line from the hole through the point where the ball last crossed the margin of the water hazard as far back as necessary so that the golfer has a line of play to advance the ball to within range of a wedge shot to the putting green. Sometimes a golfer can be seen going back 60 to 80 yards away from the creek to reach a position where the ball will clear the trees on the left and allow a fairly short shot from the point of the next position to the putting green.

One option of relief from a water hazard offers a strategic benefit. Let's say a player's ball after the

KNOWING THE RULES CAN IMPROVE YOUR SCORE

second shot on a par-5 hole has come to rest on the left side of the fairway, 20 yards from a creek that crosses the entire width of the fairway, and that the creek is identified as a water hazard by yellow stakes showing its margin. On the next shot the player hits the ball over the creek, but it bounces backward and into the water hazard. Because the ball advanced beyond the water hazard, many golfers think that they are allowed to drop on the far side of the water hazard at approximately the point where the ball came across the water hazard. In fact, that is not an option. One option that is available that may give the player a better line of play is to drop a ball along a line from the hole going back through the point where the ball last crossed the margin of the water hazard to the position where the player wants to drop. The angle of the shot toward the hole from that position may be better than if the player chose to drop a ball at the point as close as possible to where the last shot was hit.

When a ball comes to rest in either a water hazard or a lateral water hazard there is always the option of playing the ball as it lies. In the 1947 Masters Jimmy Demaret on the par-5 fifteenth hole hit his second shot over the pond in front of the green only to watch it roll back into the water. When he reached the ball he could see that it was submerged, but it was just below the waterline resting on the floor of the pond. He decided to play the ball as it lay. In order to get a stance he had to take off his shoes and socks and stand in the water. He had to be careful not to allow his club to touch the water prior to making his shot because that would have been grounding his club in a water hazard. With a furious swing he lofted the ball out of the pond and onto the green, where it came to rest only four feet from the hole. He made the putt for birdie and went on to win his second Masters that year.

Usually the margin of a lateral or water hazard is marked not only by stakes but also lines on the ground to define the margin of the hazard. That margin can be several feet away from the water in a creek or a pond. If a player chooses to hit a ball from within this margin, then that is allowed. However, even though the ball is not underwater in a water hazard, if the ball lies within the margin of the hazard the restrictions apply. The player cannot ground the club prior to the shot.

The same option of taking the ball back along a line from the hole through the point where the ball was last at rest is available in an unplayable lie situation. An example would be a hole where the tee shot goes into an area of trees along the right side of the fairway, which is adjacent to the next fairway. Rather than hacking out to the fairway you are playing, or taking a drop two club lengths from where the ball came to rest, a player can use the option to go back along a line from the hole through the position of the ball. The opportunity that option provides is to go back to a place where there are no obstructions and a good lie is available, possibly the fairway of the adjacent hole. Then the player might have a reasonable prospect of reaching the green on the next shot or advancing the ball. The one-stroke penalty incurred will be better than wasting more shots trying to advance the ball from its poor position. An example of where this option is not advantageous is when a player hits a drive left into an area of thick trees and bushes and that area is the border of the course. Going back from that point may not be an option. In that case, the best strategic option is to return to the position of the last shot, drop a ball as near to that position as possible, and hit again from there. At that time the player would be hitting the third shot: one being the first shot, two being the penalty stroke to return to the position of the original shot.

The same options regarding an unplayable lie situation are available in a bunker, with the important condition that the ball cannot be dropped outside the bunker unless the player returns to where the previous stroke was last played. That is the limit for taking the ball back along a line from the hole through the point of the original position of the ball. An example would be a ball that is lodged between the sand and the grass lip of the bunker. That is the situation that Corey Pavin faced in the 1992 U.S. Open at Pebble Beach. A ball is considered to be in a bunker when it touches the sand in the bunker or lies in the bunker. Pavin's ball was determined to be in the bunker when it became stuck between the grass surrounding a bunker and the sand in it. That meant that his options were reduced to the area of the bunker for a drop if he wanted to declare the ball unplayable and did not want to return to the spot of his previous stroke. He took a penalty stroke when he dropped the ball along a line between the hole and where the ball had originally come to rest. The option of declaring the ball unplayable and dropping it resulted in one penalty stroke, but on his next shot out of the bunker Pavin was able to advance the ball. Leaving it in its previous position might have resulted in three additional strokes to free the ball from its position, then advance the ball toward the hole.

Abnormal ground conditions such as water left on a fairway after a heavy rain allow for relief. Ground under repair on a golf course is usually identified by a white line surrounding the area so designated. An example might be where a course is repairing a drainage problem on the fairway and

93

Knowing the Rules allows a golfer to be aware of all the options available in each situation that might be encountered on a golf course. While it is always important to avoid mistakes that lead to penalties, the knowledge of every option available allows a golfer different means of advancing the ball in the fewest strokes possible.

new sod has been put in place. Rather than allow golfers to put divots in the sod, or worse, tear up entire sections of the sod when making a shot, the ground is marked as ground under repair so that golfers can take a free drop away from the area to protect the turf. If a ball enters into an abnormal ground condition through the green, then the ball can be lifted and dropped by the player no closer to the hole within one club length of the nearest point of relief of the original position of the ball. If the ball enters into an abnormal ground condition in a bunker, then it must remain in the bunker after the drop. On the putting green the relief from an abnormal ground condition is to place the ball at the nearest point of relief, as opposed to dropping it.

Knowing the Rules allows a golfer to be aware of all the options available in each situation that might be encountered on a golf course. While it is always important to avoid mistakes that lead to penalties, the knowledge of every option available allows a golfer different means of advancing the ball in the

94

fewest strokes possible. That is where strategic thinking becomes important, because it is frequently the golfer's choice which option to use. The Rules do not say "do this first," or "next try this," and "then this." It is up to the player to determine which available relief will provide the most benefit and then proceed as dictated by the Rules.

12

The Evolution of the Rules

The exact date when golf first was played in Scotland is not known, though the game goes back at least 700 years. A variant of the game had been played in Holland for several hundred years prior to its development in Scotland. What is known is the date of the first published set of Rules, March of 1744, which numbered only 13. These were prepared to regulate a competition over the Links at Leith, near Edinburgh, Scotland. Many of the Rules established at that time still apply to the game today, but it is worthwhile to appreciate that the Rules change over time in response to developments in equipment—or, as described today, technology, course design, playing conditions, player ability, and other factors.

The first of those original 13 Rules, "You must Tee your Ball within a Club's length of the Hole," is no longer part of the game. Imagine dropping a ball a club length from the hole on the twelfth putting green at Augusta National and then hitting a drive up the fairway of the thirteenth hole. Any disruption of the turf would be the tough luck of whoever played in the next group. Sand was used to create a tee in the early years of the game, which was left on the putting green after the golfer hit the tee shot. Putting through that sand pile would not be fun for the other golfers if it lay in the line of their putt to the hole. In today's game a smooth surface is expected whenever putting, and some provisions are made in the Rules of Golf to assure that a golfer does not confront impediments to sinking a putt, such as pitch marks from previous shots, an unclean golf ball, or a ball sitting in the line of a putt, a situ-

> In today's game a smooth surface is expected whenever putting, and some provisions are made in the Rules of Golf to assure that a golfer does not confront impediments to sinking a putt, such as pitch marks from previous shots, an unclean golf ball, or a ball sitting in the line of a putt, a situation known as a *stymie*, which was part of the Rules until 1952.

ation known as a stymie, which was part of the Rules until 1952.

The stymie played a critical part in one of the game's greatest accomplishments: Bobby Jones's Grand Slam, in 1930. At the British Amateur that year Jones faced Cyril Tolley in his fourth round match at the Old Course at St. Andrews. They tied after the regulation 18-hole match-play round. On the first playoff hole Tolley lay three after his drive, an approach shot to the left of the green, and a chip to seven feet from the hole. Jones was on in two, 10 feet from the hole, so he putted first. He left his approach putt, his third shot on the hole, in the path of Tolley's access to the hole, making it necessary for Tolley to chip over Jones's ball to have any hope of sinking his shot. He didn't hole out, and Jones won the hole and the match when he sank his short putt. He went on to win his first and only British Amateur championship, the first leg of what became known as the Grand Slam. Jones thought that the stymie was an integral part of the game, and he protested the elimination of the stymie from 1951 through the rest of his life.

One result of the Rules of Golf being more favorable for putting in today's game than in previous eras is fewer putts in a round of golf. Certainly better turf conditions and more consistent putting green surfaces contribute to better putting, but even Bobby Jones recognized that putting had improved by the late 1950s since his competitive era of the 1920s. "Whereas we used to consider an average of 32 or 33 putts per round to represent a quite acceptable performance for the winner of a championship, now it is not uncommon to see this number reduced to 28, 27, or even occasionally to 26," he wrote in *Bobby Jones On Golf*. "The resulting effect upon scoring is obvious. At times, I find myself mildly, even though enviously, amused by the agonies expressed before television cameras when some players fail to hole out from 25 or 30 feet. Most of my contemporaries were well pleased if from such distances they could consistently roll the ball close enough to the cup to make certain of holing the next one."

The Rules of the game of golf change over time in some aspects and that affects scores, but the basic character of the game has not changed. A review of the other Rules established in 1744 shows how much the game has retained its original character. (The spelling is in the original text.)

Rule 2: *Your Tee must be upon the Ground.*

Rule 3: *You are not to change the Ball which you Strike off the Tee.*

Rule 4: *You are not to remove, Stones, Bones or any Break Club for the sake of playing your Ball, Except upon the fair Green & that only within a Club's length of your Ball.*

Rule 5: *If your Ball comes among Watter, or any Wattery Filth, you are at liberty to take out your Ball & bringing it behind the hazard and Teeing it, you may play it with any Club and allow your Adversary a Stroke for so getting out your Ball.*

Rule 6: *If your Balls be found anywhere touching one another, You are to lift the first Ball, till you play the last.*

Rule 7: *At Holling, you are to play your Ball honestly for the Hole, and, not to play upon your Adversary's Ball, not lying in your way to the Hole.*

Rule 8: *If you shou'd lose your Ball, by its being taken up, or any other way, you are to go back to the Spot, where you struck your last & drop another Ball, And Allow your Adversary a Stroke for the misfortune.*

Rule 9: *No man at Holling his Ball, is to be allowed, to mark his way to the Hole with his Club or, any thing else.*

Rule 10: *If a Ball be stopp'd by any person, Horse, Dog, or any thing else, The Ball so stopp'd must be play'd where it lyes.*

Rule 11: *If you draw your Club, in order to Strike & proceed so far in the Stroke, as to be bringing down your Club; if then, your Club shall break, in any way, it is to be Accounted a Stroke.*

Rule 12: *He, whose Ball lyes farthest from the Hole, is obliged to play first.*

Rule 13: *Neither Trench, Ditch, or Dyke, made for the preservation of the Links, nor the Scholar's Holes or the Soldier's Lines, Shall be accounted a Hazard; But the Ball is to be taken out Teed and play'd with any Iron Club.*

The last Rule in this list would today be considered a local rule, applicable only to a specific course. Rules 2 through 12 are still part of the game. The second Rule from 1744 may be considered different from today when a tee can be used to place the ball above the ground. Given that teeing the ball in that earlier era meant building a mound of sand to set up the ball, without any unusual artificial material, then the tee of today would be the equivalent of the small mound of sand. It's just a different material. Also, the fact that there are now teeing grounds as opposed to teeing off from a position one club length from the hole, and that the wooden tee is a more practical solution as to how to tee the ball, makes the evolution of this Rule more understandable.

Rule 3 from 1744 is essentially the current Rule 15-1 in the Rules of Golf: A player must hole out with the ball played from the teeing ground unless a Rule permits him to substitute another ball. Rule 4 correlates with the current Rule 23 (Loose Impediments). Rule 5 from 1744 addresses the circumstances that are covered by Rule 25 today

(Abnormal Ground Conditions) and Rule 26 (Water Hazards).

Rule 6 from 1744 was modified in 1775 to read: "If your Balls be found anywhere touching or within six inches of one another, you are to lift the first Ball until the other is played." Thus, if a player's ball was more than six inches from another player's ball on the putting green no relief was available. However the shot needed to be made to negotiate around the ball in the path to the hole, that was how the shot was to be played—thus, the stymie.

Rule 7 from 1744 regarding hitting toward the hole as opposed to hitting to deflect or otherwise affect your adversary's ball doesn't have much application today. It would be an unusual situation to benefit from hitting one's ball into another player's ball. In an earlier time, however, it was as though an element of croquet was being prohibited. Rule 8 is now found in Rule 27 (Ball Lost or Out of Bounds). Rule 9 relates to the current Rule 8 (Indicating Line of Play).

Today anyone who has played the Old Course at St. Andrews can appreciate Rule 10 from 1744, other than the unlikely appearance of a horse on the links. Even that sight would not have been unusual until the twentieth century. Even today pedestrians cross the first and eighteenth fairways of the course on a regular basis, and this Rule addresses what should be done in the case of hitting someone, human or animal, crossing the golf course. Today's Rule 19 (Ball in Motion Deflected or Stopped) discusses this situation.

The transition from wooden shafted clubs to steel shafts in the late 1920s and early 1930s reduced the frequency of broken golf clubs, which Rule 11 in 1744 addressed. Today's Rule 14 (Striking the Ball) discusses this situation. Something that hasn't changed from 1744 through today is the order of play: The ball farthest from the hole shall be played first. The earlier Rule 12 is now covered by Rule 10 (Order of Play), but there is no alteration of the meaning of this rule.

> The most important aspect of the game is still the principle of playing the ball as it lies. Though that was not specifically stated as part of the Rules in 1744, that concept is as basic to golf today as it was 250 years ago.

What can be seen from looking at the brief list of Rules in 1744 is that consideration was given for the way in which different ground conditions or terrain affect the playing of the game (loose impediments, water, lost ball, ball deflected by an outside agency). An emphasis on the player's not receiving advantage (by marking the way to the hole, or getting relief even when an outside agency affects the movement of the ball) can be seen as an element of the game that has survived to the current era. The most important aspect of the game is still the principle of playing the ball as it lies. Though that was not specifically stated as part of the Rules in 1744, that concept is as basic to golf today as it was 250 years ago. The Rules may have evolved in terms of clarification and elaboration of what to do under nearly every possible circumstance on a golf course. The process of getting the ball in the hole in the fewest number of strokes has not changed dramatically, nor has the responsibility of each golfer to monitor his or her compliance with the Rules. A golfer who learns the Rules and plays by them becomes part of a tradition and legacy going back hundreds of years, a worthwhile endeavor.

The Rules and the Majors

Four events have become recognized over the past century of competitive golf as the most significant in the men's game: The Masters, the U.S. Open, the Open Championship (The British Open), and the PGA Championship. The Masters didn't begin play until 1934, and so it is the youngest of these events. It is called a tournament because, as Bob Jones rightly pointed out, if it were called a championship, of what entity would it be the championship? The U.S. Open for men is the championship of the USGA. The Open Championship is conducted by the R&A, whose offices are in St. Andrews, Scotland. The PGA Championship is conducted by the PGA of America, not to be confused with the PGA Tour.

Each of these events attracts the best golfers chasing the coveted winner's trophy, and no career in professional golf is considered complete without at least one victory in a major. Complications with the Rules in the majors usually don't affect the primary contenders, but when it happens, it is always remembered, because the Rules situation either nearly cost someone a major win or, despite the issue, the player went on to victory. Given the importance of the majors, these incidents continue to have prominence in the lore of golf.

Bob Jones's career had several pivotal episodes where the Rules affected the outcome of his performance in a major. At the age of 19 in 1921 Jones played in the Open Championship at St. Andrews. In the third round by the ninth hole he had already accumulated 46 strokes—an uncharacteristic performance for him. He then double bogeyed the tenth hole. What happened next even Jones recounted in different published versions. In his book *Down the Fairway*, which appeared in 1927, he stated that after five shots he was on the green of the par-3 eleventh hole, trying to putt to save a triple bogey, which would have put him at 15 over par for the round. He claimed he picked up his ball before putting. In the version of the incident he wrote for *Golf Is My Game*, which appeared 30 years later, he described picking up his ball in a bunker. In both scenarios, he withdrew from the competition. What is known is that he turned in his card for the third round and played in the fourth round, though he is listed as having withdrawn from the event after the second round. He considered his antics in the third round to be his most embarrassing behavior as a competitive golfer, later describing that day as "the most inglorious failure of my golfing life."

His temper also brought him the ire of the USGA. In a U.S. Amateur Championship Jones, in a tantrum, threw a club that hit a female spectator. The president of the USGA warned Jones in a letter that he would be prohibited from playing in USGA events if he did not improve his sportsmanship. Both the Open Championship withdrawal and the club-throwing episode can be considered breaches of etiquette. If Jones had not learned to control his temper, he might never have accomplished what he did. How Jones admirably handled a Rules situation in another event still defines the character of the man. At the 1925 U.S. Open in the first round Jones saw his ball move when he brushed the grass alongside his ball during a practice stroke. He called a penalty stroke on himself, despite the protestations of Rules officials and spectators who said they did not see the ball move. He went on to a 36-hole playoff against Willie Macfarlane, which Jones lost. Praised afterward for what he had done regarding the moving ball infraction, Jones replied, "You might as well praise a man for not robbing a bank." Jones is remembered today as much for how he finally overcame his bad temper on the golf course and his strict adherence to the Rules as he is for his accomplishments in competitive golf.

Byron Nelson won the 1939 U.S. Open, the Masters in 1937 and 1942, and the PGA Championship in 1940 and 1945, along with more than 50 other PGA Tour events. A Rules issue cost him a penalty stroke at the 1946 U.S. Open, although he himself was not responsible for it. That penalty stoke contributed to Nelson ending in a tie for the lead after four rounds, facing Lloyd Mangrum and Vic Ghezzi in a playoff. At that time, the crowds of spectators were not contained from the fairways during a competition by ropes along the sides of the course as they are now, the exceptions in Nelson's era being the PGA Championship and the Masters. Between shots, fans could stroll the fairways alongside the players. In the third round Nelson's caddy was trying to reach the ball after the second shot on the par-5 thirteenth hole. The crowd was gathering around where the ball lay, and marshalls were beginning to rope off the area immediately near the ball to allow Nelson room to make his swing. As Nelson's caddy dipped under the rope he stumbled and kicked Nelson's ball, moving it a foot, resulting in the penalty stroke. By his own admission the incident rattled Nelson sufficiently that he shot two over par coming in for the third round but still ended after the fourth round tied with Lloyd Mangrum and Vic Ghezzi. Mangrum won the playoff.

When Roberto De Vicenzo came into contention at the Masters in 1968 it was not surprising. He had won the Open Championship in 1967 at age 44 and seemed to be at the top of his game after 20 years as a touring pro. In the final round of the 1968 Masters he shot a blistering 65 to apparently tie Bob Goalby for the lead and forcing a playoff. De Vicenzo's playing partner for the day, responsible for marking down De Vicenzo's score, posted a 4 instead of the 3 De Vicenzo made on the seventeenth hole. De Vicenzo did not notice the error, signed his card, and turned it in. As a consequence, the incorrect 4 resulted in De Vicenzo having a 66 in the final round and Goalby won the tournament. De Vicenzo finished second. Even Bob Jones was consulted about what should be done in the situation and Jones stated that there was no choice other than to follow the applicable Rule.

Less well known was a situation in which De Vicenzo properly used a Rule for his benefit in the Open Championship at Troon in 1950, a year he eventually finished second. At that time the R&A and the USGA did not have complete compliance on the Rules. Several of the penalties for infractions of the Rules were less punitive in the R&A's version of the Rules. On the eighth hole in the third round De Vicenzo hit his tee shot into a bunker on the short par-3 hole known as the "postage stamp" for its small green. Declaring his ball unplayable, he hit another shot from the tee, made the putt, and took a par on the hole. Under the then-current Rules issued by the R&A the penalty for an unplayable lie was only distance, with no penalty stroke added to the score as was the case under USGA Rules then in effect. Because of such divergences there was collaboration between the USGA and the R&A so that the Rules could conform to one standard, which was achieved for 1952 and thereafter.

In the 1991 PGA Championship, ninth-alternate player John Daly appeared to be on his way to one of the most improbable wins ever in major championship history after opening with rounds of 69 and 67. In the third round, on the eleventh green, it appeared that Daly's caddie had touched the flagstick to the green on the line of Daly's putt, a breach of Rule 8-2b. After reviewing videotape of the episode the rules officials determined there was no infraction and Daly's birdie on the hole would stand. He went on despite the distraction to shoot 69 that day and 71 in the final round to win.

The PGA Championship of 2010 was the scene of another unfortunate Rules incident that follows the theme of breaches of the Rules in the majors almost invariably being caused by a player's ignorance about how to proceed in a given situation, rather than any deliberate attempt to compromise the Rules. Dustin Johnson had a one-shot lead coming to the eighteenth hole at Whistling Straights. His tee shot veered right and up a slope among the spectators, resting in a sandy area. When the crowd moved away and Johnson approached his ball, the fact that the crowd had just previously been standing along that ground provided an impression that although the area was sandy, it was not a sand bunker. "Walking up there, seeing the shot, it never once crossed my mind that I was in a sand trap," Johnson said after the Championship was over. When he set up to hit his shot, he grounded his 4-iron in the sand behind the ball. He hit his shot and ultimately bogeyed the hole, which he thought would put him in a playoff. But when he was leaving the green a Rules official informed him that grounding his club in a hazard cost him a two-stroke penalty. Instead of joining Martin Kaymer and Bubba Watson for that playoff, Johnson finished two strokes out of the lead, putting him in fifth place.

Many viewers of Johnson's fate sympathized with him and claimed that golf is an unfair game. Yet how the sandy areas would be treated in the Championship was addressed by The PGA of America with notices posted in the locker room and on the first tee throughout the week, reminding players that all bunkers would be treated like hazards, all several hundred of them at Whistling Straits.

One of the key principles of the Rules of Golf is that of equity. Like situations or circumstances on a golf course as a player goes through a round are to be treated with identical options or penalties, whatever the case may be. "I wasn't aware of that rule," is not a legitimate excuse in golf, especially not in tournament golf when a golfer can request assistance from a rules official to determine the proper options in any given situation before making a shot. Looking at the entire history of the majors, when there have been ample opportunities for mistakes, it is remarkable that so few Rules' matters have affected the outcome of who won each year.

Summary of Penalties

- Hitting your equipment with your ball: one stroke
- Carrying more than 14 clubs: two strokes for each hole the player had the clubs, with a maximum of four strokes
- Hitting outside the teeing ground: in stroke play, two strokes (player must tee off again from within the teeing ground)
- Moving the tee markers: two strokes
- Providing advice on club selection or the golf swing: two penalty strokes
- Ball moved during a search: one stroke (moved ball must be replaced)
- Ball moved during practice swing: one stroke (moved ball must be replaced)
- Altering the golf course: two strokes
- Unplayable ball: one stroke
- Hitting the wrong ball: two penalty strokes (return to original point and play correct ball)
- Lost ball: one stroke (return to original position and play another ball)

- Touching the sand prior to shot: two strokes
- Removing loose impediments from a bunker: two strokes
- Ball out of bounds: one stroke (return to original point for next shot)
- Improving the line of a putt: two strokes
- Ball putted on the green hits another ball: two strokes
- Playing from the wrong place: two strokes

For Further Reading

Understanding how the Rules of Golf developed over time allows for better appreciation of why the game is played the way it is. *The Rules of the Green: A History of the Rules of Golf* by Kenneth G. Chapman (Triumph Books) reviews how the game changed over time and then provides a rule-by-rule analysis of how each rule has changed. *The Historical Dictionary of Golfing Terms* (Michael Kesend Publishing) not only serves as a glossary of the words used in golf, but most of the entries have quotes that illustrate how the term has been used in different eras of the game. *Playing by the Rules* by Arnold Palmer (Pocket Books) gives a personal perspective on the Rules of the game with many anecdotes from Palmer's career as well as situations that he has observed. Gary Galyean's book *Golf Rules Illustrated* (Hamlyn) is comprehensive in its discussion of the Rules, including match play, the administration of competitions, and the conditions of competition. *The Rules of Golf* as published by the USGA is the most complete and definitive version of the Rules, but the

USGA's website (www.rulesofgolf.com) also provides answers to specific Rules situations and information on the various publications that can assist in understanding how the game should be played. *Golf Etiquette* (St. Martin's Press) by Barbara Puett and Jim Apfelbaum discusses in a humorous style everything from what to wear to taking lessons.

Index

Page numbers in *italics* refer to photographs and/or their captions.

119

123

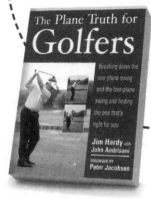